T0018961

Learn a Language!

See and Say
French

by Golriz Golkar

CAPSTONE PRESS
a capstone imprint

Published by Pebble, an imprint of Capstone
1710 Roe Crest Drive, North Mankato, Minnesota 56003
capstonepub.com

Copyright © 2025 by Capstone. All rights reserved. No part of this publication may be reproduced in whole or in part, or stored in a retrieval system, or transmitted in any form or by any means, electronic, mechanical, photocopying, recording, or otherwise, without written permission of the publisher.

Library of Congress Cataloging-in-Publication Data is available on the Library of Congress website.

ISBN: 9780756581763 (hardcover)
ISBN: 9780756581824 (paperback)
ISBN: 9780756581800 (ebook PDF)

Summary: How do you greet someone in French? What's the French word for *horse*? With this book, curious kids will see and say simple words and phrases in French.

Editorial Credits
Editor: Ericka Smith; Designer: Sarah Bennett; Media Researcher: Svetlana Zhurkin; Production Specialist: Katy LaVigne

Image Credits
Alamy: BSIP SA, 18 (middle right); Getty Images: GoodLifeStudio, 6, Jupiterimages, 7 (top), Khosrork, 7 (bottom right), larik_malasha, 5 (middle right), 10 (top), loops7, 26 (bottom), martin-dm, 7 (middle), Michael Russell, 4, ozgurdonmaz, 7 (bottom left), Rubberball/Mike Kemp, 17 (middle left), SDI Productions, 23 (top), Sylvain Sonnet, 18 (middle left), Westend61, 14 (bottom); Shutterstock: Africa Studio, 22 (bottom), AlexeiLogvinovich, 12 (bottom left), Alphapicto, 18 (top), Anna Andersson Fotografi, 14 (top), Antoine2K, 26 (top), Apiwan Borrikonratchata, 13 (top left), asife, 31 (middle), Atlaspix, cover (middle left), BearFotos, 21 (bottom), bellena, 19 (middle), bergamont, 29 (middle right), Boonchuay Promjiam, 29 (bottom left), Brent Hofacker, 11 (top), Cassiohabib, 23 (middle), Creativa Images, cover (top left), daniiD, 17 (bottom), defotoberg, 18 (bottom), Dmitry Epov, 11 (middle right), Ekaterina Pokrovsky, 25 (bottom right), Elena Elisseeva, 15 (bottom), Elizabeth_0102, 29 (middle left), EQRoy, 19 (top right), 21 (top), Eric Isselee, cover (bottom left), 13 (top right), ESB Professional, 9 (top), FamVeld, 30 (middle left), Fascinadora, 30 (middle), Fotofermer, 28 (bottom left), GaudiLab, 15 (middle), goodluz, 9 (bottom), Ground Picture, 15 (top), halimqd (speech bubble and burst), cover and throughout, Irina Wilhauk, 31 (top), Ja Crispy, 12 (top left), Leitenberger Photography, 19 (top left), LiliGraphie, 25 (bottom left), Ma. Amanda A.S. Gana, 19 (bottom), Magnia (lined texture), cover and throughout, Maks Narodenko, cover (top right), MaraZe, 11 (middle left), Marc Bruxelle, 20 (middle), Margo Harrison, 13 (bottom), Maria Svetlychnaja, 16 (bottom), Milan Vachal, 18 (middle), Muenchbach, 17 (top), Naypong Studio, 29 (top), Neirfy, 5 (middle left), 25 (top right), Nina Buday, 27 (top), nukeaf, 24, oksana2010, 28 (top right), Oleg Medvedytskov, 27 (bottom), Olga Ermolaeva 84, 22 (middle), Oliver Foerstner, 26 (middle), olrat, 20 (bottom), Pack-Shot, 21 (middle), pakornkrit, 12 (top right), pikselstock, 8, Pixel-Shot, 16 (top), Porntanapat Jaisamarnmit, 13 (middle right), prapann, 12 (bottom right), Rohit Seth, cover (bottom right), 1, Roman Samborskyi, 5 (top), 23 (bottom), RossHelen, 20 (top), Ruth Black, 30 (top, middle right, and bottom), 31 (middle right, middle left, and bottom), SanRan, 25 (top left), spiharu.u (spot line art), cover and throughout, stockyimages, 17 (middle right), Tim UR, 28 (top left), timsimages, 11 (bottom), Tom Wang, 22 (top), travellight, 10 (bottom), Tsekhmister, 13 (middle left), Vangert, 28 (bottom right), winphong, 29 (bottom right)

Any additional websites and resources referenced in this book are not maintained, authorized, or sponsored by Capstone. All product and company names are trademarks™ or registered® trademarks of their respective holders.

Printed and bound in China. PO5834

Table of Contents

The French Language

The first known text to include French words was written more than 1,000 years ago. By the early 2000s, more than 25 countries had French as an official language. And for more than 122 million people around the world, French was the first or second language they learned to speak.

An official language is a language that many people in a country speak. It might be used by the government, at schools, and in other important places.

How to Use This Book

Some words and phrases complete a sentence.
Those will appear in bold.

`English` **I like . . .**
`French` J'aime . . .
`Say It!` 🐱 ZHEM

+

`English` **dancing.**
`French` danser.
`Say It!` 🐱 dahn-SEH

Others give you the name for a person,
place, thing, or idea.

`English` spring
`French` le printemps
`Say It!` 🐱 luh PRAN-tom

`English` croissant
`French` croissant
`Say It!` 🐱 kwa-SAHN

Meet Chatty Cat! Chatty Cat will show you how
to say the words and phrases in this book.

Greetings and Phrases

French Des Salutations et des Phrases

Say It! 🐱 deh sal-yoo-tah-shohn eh deh frahz

English Hello!

French Bonjour!

Say It! 🐱 bohn-zhoor

English My name is . . .

French Je m'appelle . . .

Say It! 🐱 zhuh mah-pel

English What's your name?

French Comment tu t'appelles?

Say It! 🐱 koh-mahn too tah-pel

English How are you?

French Comment ça va?

Say It! 🐱 koh-mahn sah vah

English I am fine.

French Je vais bien.

Say It! 🐱 zhuh vey byen

English Nice to meet you.

French Ravi de te rencontrer. (a boy speaking)

Ravie de te rencontrer. (a girl speaking)

Say It! 🐱 rah-vee duh tuh rohn-kohn-treh

English Please.
French S'il te plaît.
Say It! 🐱 seel tuh play

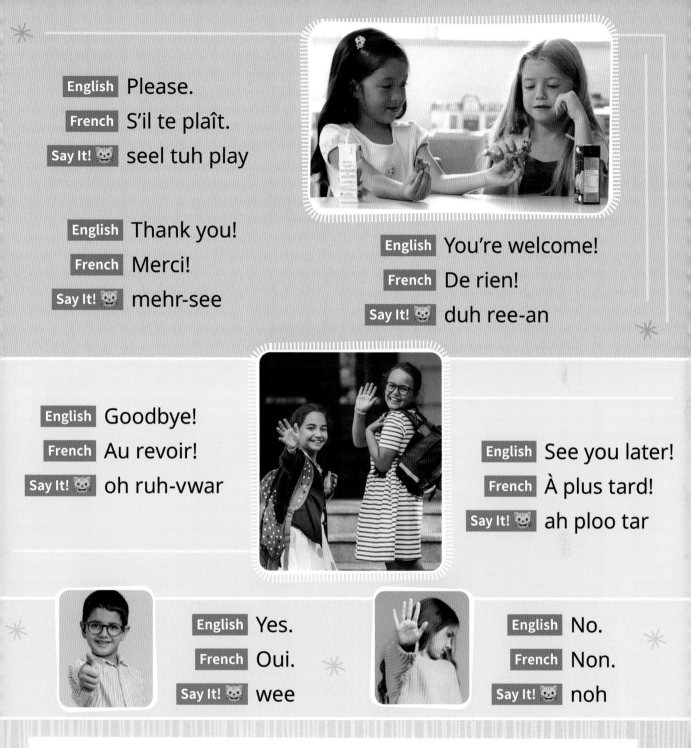

English Thank you!
French Merci!
Say It! 🐱 mehr-see

English You're welcome!
French De rien!
Say It! 🐱 duh ree-an

English Goodbye!
French Au revoir!
Say It! 🐱 oh ruh-vwar

English See you later!
French À plus tard!
Say It! 🐱 ah ploo tar

English Yes.
French Oui.
Say It! 🐱 wee

English No.
French Non.
Say It! 🐱 noh

Greetings in French change during different times of the day. *Bonjour* is a common way to greet someone at any time. You may also say *bon après-midi* (bohn ah-pray-mee-dee) in the afternoon ("good afternoon") and *bonsoir* (bohn-swar) in the evening ("good evening").

Family

English **This is . . .**
French C'est . . .
Say It! 🐱 seh

English **my mother.**
French ma mère.
Say It! 🐱 mah mehr

English **my father.**
French mon père.
Say It! 🐱 mohn pehr

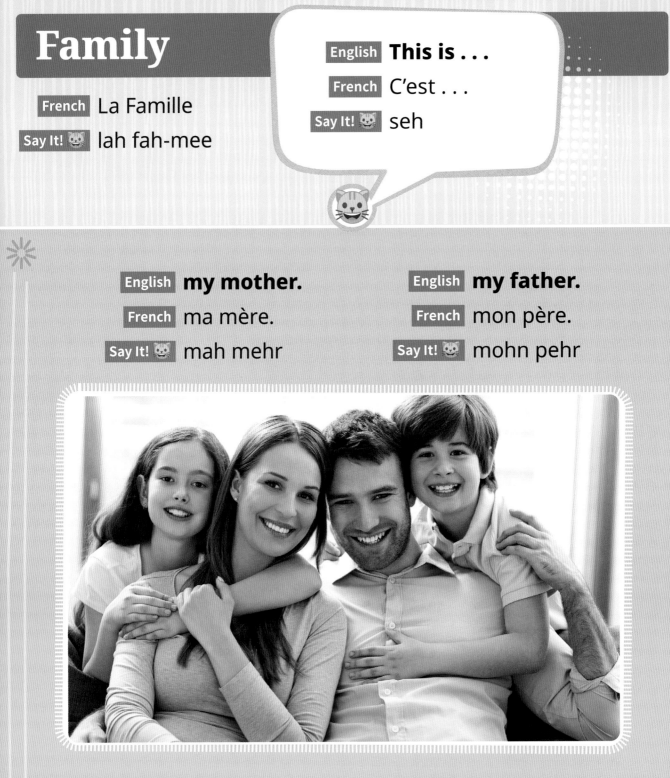

English **my sister.**
French ma soeur.
Say It! 🐱 mah sur

English **my brother.**
French mon frère.
Say It! 🐱 mohn frehr

English	my aunt.
French	ma tante.
Say It! 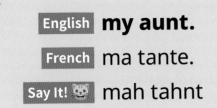	mah tahnt

English	my uncle.
French	mon oncle.
Say It! 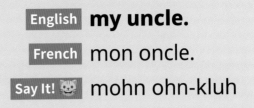	mohn ohn-kluh

English	my cousin.
French	mon cousin. (boy)
Say It!	mohn koo-zan
French	ma cousine. (girl)
Say It!	mah koo-zeen

English	my grandfather.
French	mon grand-père.
Say It!	mohn grahn-pehr

English	my grandmother.
French	ma grand-mère.
Say It! 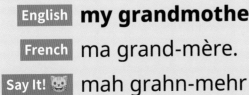	mah grahn-mehr

Food

French La Nourriture
Say It! lah noo-ree-toor

English **I'm hungry. I want . . .**
French J'ai faim. Je veux . . .
Say It! zhay fam zhuh vuh

English **breakfast.**
French le petit-déjeuner.
Say It! luh puh-tee day-zhuh-nay

English chocolate croissant
French pain au chocolat
Say It! pan oh shoh-ko-lah

English croissant
French croissant
Say It! kwa-sahn

English **lunch.**
French le déjeuner.
Say It! luh day-zhuh-nay

English quiche
French quiche
Say It! keesh

English a green salad
French une salade verte
Say It! oon sah-lahd vehrt

English **dinner.**
French le dîner.
Say It!  luh dee-neh

English steak and fries
French steak frites
Say It! stake freet

English **a snack.**
French un goûter.
Say It! uhn goo-teh

English cherries
French des cerises
Say It! deh sur-eez

English milk
French lait
Say It! lay

English bread
French pain
Say It! pan

Many French people do not eat a cooked meal for breakfast. Instead, they go to a *boulangerie* (boo-lahn-zhuh-ree), a bakery, or a restaurant for a pastry or a *tartine* (tar-teen), bread with butter and jam.

Animals

English a cat

French un chat

Say It! 🐱 uhn shah

English a dog

French un chien

Say It! 🐱 uhn shehn

English a horse

French un cheval

Say It! 🐱 uhn shuh-vahl

English a chicken

French un poulet

Say It! 🐱 uhn poo-leh

English a fish
French un poisson
Say It! 🐱 uhn pwah-sohn

English a bird
French un oiseau
Say It! 🐱 uhn wa-zoh

English a pig
French un cochon
Say It! 🐱 uhn ko-shohn

English a frog
French une grenouille
Say It! 🐱 oon gruh-noo-yuh

English a cow
French une vache
Say It! 🐱 oon vash

At Home

French À la Maison

Say It! 🐱 ah lah meh-zohn

English a kitchen

French une cuisine

Say It! 🐱 oon kwee-zeen

English a table

French une table

Say It! 🐱 oon tah-bluh

English a chair

French une chaise

Say It! 🐱 oon shez

English a couch

French un canapé

Say It! 🐱 uhn kan-uh-peh

English a living room

French un salon

Say It! 🐱 uhn sah-lohn

English a door

French une porte

Say It! 🐱 oon pohrt

English a window

French une fenêtre

Say It! 🐱 oon fuh-neh-truh

English a computer

French un ordinateur

Say It! 🐱 uhn or-dee-nah-tur

English a bedroom
French une chambre
Say It! 🐱 oon shahm-bruh

English a bed
French un lit
Say It! 🐱 uhn lee

English a cell phone
French un téléphone portable
Say It! 🐱 uhn tel-uh-fohn por-tah-bluh

English a bathroom
French une salle de bain
Say It! 🐱 oon sahl duh ban

English a sink
French un lavabo
Say It! 🐱 uhn lah-vah-boh

English a bathtub
French une baignoire
Say It! 🐱 oon ben-war

English the toilet
French des toilettes
Say It! 🐱 deh twa-let

Clothing

English I am wearing . . .
French Je porte . . .
Say It! 🐱 zhuh port

English a shirt.
French une chemise.
Say It! 🐱 oon shuh-meez

English pants.
French un pantalon.
Say It! 🐱 uhn pawn-tah-lohn

English a hat.
French un chapeau.
Say It! 🐱 uhn sha-poh

English a coat.
French un manteau.
Say It! 🐱 uhn mahn-tow

16

English **a sweatshirt.**
French un pull.
Say It! 🐱 uhn puhl

English **a dress.**
French une robe.
Say It! 🐱 oon rohb

English **socks.**
French des chaussettes.
Say It! 🐱 deh shoh-set

English **a skirt.**
French une jupe.
Say It! 🐱 oon zhoop

English **shoes.**
French des chaussures.
Say It! 🐱 deh shoh-soor

17

In the Neighborhood

French Dans le Quartier

Say It! 🐱 dahn luh car-tyeh

English an apartment

French un appartement

Say It! 🐱 uhn uh-par-tuh-mahn

English a house

French une maison

Say It! 🐱 oon meh-zohn

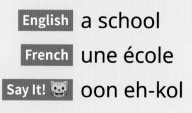

English a park

French un parc

Say It! 🐱 uhn park

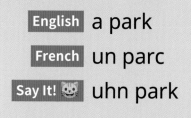

English a school

French une école

Say It! 🐱 oon eh-kol

English a grocery store

French un supermarché

Say It! 🐱 uhn soo-per-mar-sheh

English a hospital

French un hôpital

Say It! 🐱 uhn oh-pee-tahl

English a post office

French un bureau de poste

Say It! 🐱 uhn byoo-roh duh pohst

English a library

French une bibliothèque

Say It! 🐱 oon beeb-lee-oh-tek

English a bus stop

French un arrêt de bus

Say It! 🐱 uhn ar-eh duh bewss

English a street

French une rue

Say It! 🐱 oon roo

English a swimming pool

French une piscine

Say It! 🐱 oon pee-seen

Public swimming pools are very popular in France year-round. People go to pools to swim for fun or to take swimming lessons.

19

Transportation

French Les Transports

Say It! 🐱 leh trahn-spohr

English a boat

French un bateau

Say It! 🐱 uhn bah-toh

English a bus

French un bus

Say It! 🐱 uhn bewss

English a bicycle

French un vélo

Say It! 🐱 uhn veh-loh

English a train

French un train

Say It! 🐱 uhn tran

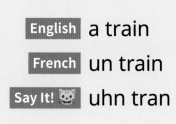

English an airplane
French un avion
Say It! uhn ah-vee-ohn

English a truck
French un camion
Say It! uhn kam-ee-ohn

English a car
French une voiture
Say It! oon vwah-toor

English the subway
French le métro
Say It! luh meh-troh

Some big cities in France have great subway systems. Paris has 16 connected lines that take travelers all around the city. Many French people take the subway to and from work and school every day.

21

Hobbies

French **Les Loisirs**

Say It! 🐱 leh luah-zeer

English **I like . . .**

French J'aime . . .

Say It! 🐱 zhem

English **singing.**

French chanter.

Say It! 🐱 shahn-teh

English **drawing.**

French dessiner.

Say It! 🐱 deh-see-neh

English **reading.**

French lire.

Say It! 🐱 leer

English books

French des livres

Say It! 🐱 deh lee-vruh

English **playing soccer.**
French jouer au foot.
Say It! 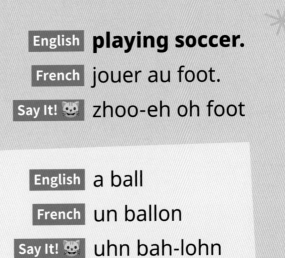 zhoo-eh oh foot

English a ball
French un ballon
Say It! uhn bah-lohn

English **swimming**.
French nager.
Say It!  nah-jeh

English **dancing.**
French danser.
Say It! dahn-seh

23

Days of the Week

French Les Jours de la Semaine

Say It!  leh zhoor duh lah suh-men

English Today is . . .

French Aujourd'hui c'est . . .

Say It! oh-joord-wee seh

English **Monday.**

French Lundi.

Say It! lun-dee

English **Tuesday.**

French Mardi.

Say It! mar-dee

English **Wednesday.**

French Mercredi.

Say It! mehr-cruh-dee

English **Thursday.**

French Jeudi.

Say It! zhuh-dee

English **Friday.**

French Vendredi.

Say It! vahn-druh-dee

English **Saturday.**

French Samedi.

Say It! sam-dee

English **Sunday.**

French Dimanche.

Say It! dee-mahnsh

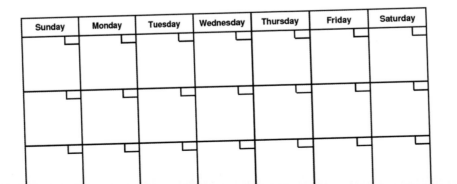

Sunday	Monday	Tuesday	Wednesday	Thursday	Friday	Saturday

Seasons

French Les Saisons

Say It! 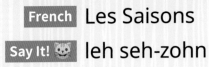 leh seh-zohn

English winter

French l'hiver

Say It!  lee-vehr

English spring

French le printemps

Say It! luh pran-tom

English summer

French l'été

Say It! leh-teh

English fall

French l'automne

Say It!  loh-tohm

25

Weather

French La Météo
Say It! 🐱 lah meh-teh-yo

English It . . .
French Il . . .
Say It! 🐱 eel

English **is raining.**
French pleut.
Say It! 🐱 pluh

English **is windy.**
French fait du vent.
Say It! 🐱 feh doo vahn

English **is cold.**
French fait froid.
Say It! 🐱 feh fwah

English **is snowing.**
French neige.
Say It! 🐱 nezh

26

English **is hot.**
French fait chaud.
Say It! 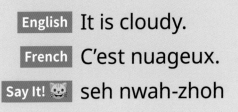 feh shoh

English **is sunny.**
French y a du soleil.
Say It! yah doo soh-lay

English It is cloudy.
French C'est nuageux.
Say It! seh nwah-zhoh

Colors

English red

French rouge

Say It! 🐱 roozh

English pink

French rose

Say It! 🐱 rohz

English green

French vert

Say It! 🐱 vehr

English orange

French orange

Say It! 🐱 or-ahnzh

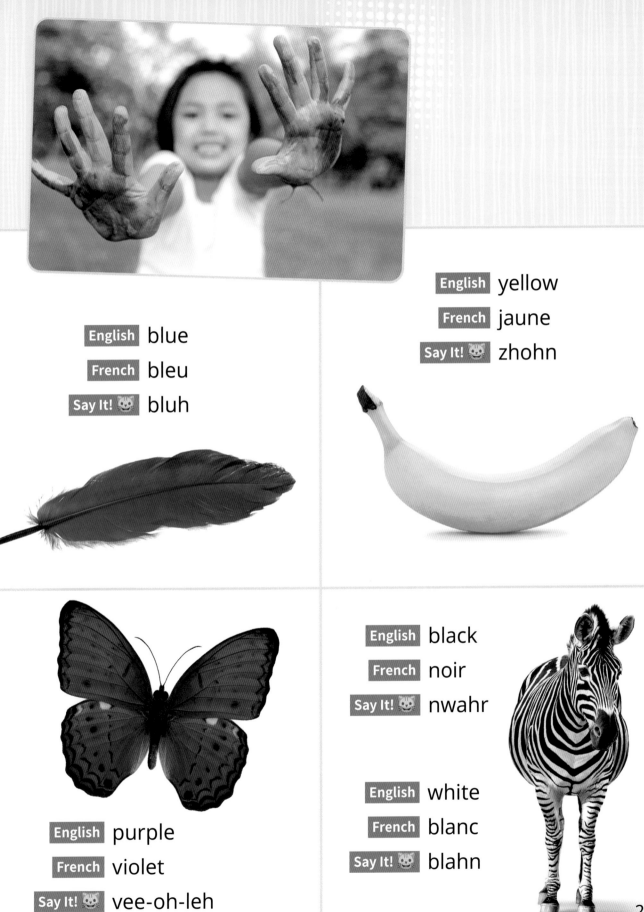

English yellow
French jaune
Say It! 🐱 zhohn

English blue
French bleu
Say It! 🐱 bluh

English black
French noir
Say It! 🐱 nwahr

English white
French blanc
Say It! 🐱 blahn

English purple
French violet
Say It! 🐱 vee-oh-leh

Numbers

French Les Chiffres

Say It! 🐱 leh sheef-ruh

1

English one

French un

Say It! 🐱 uhn

2

English two

French deux

Say It! 🐱 duh

3

English three

French trois

Say It! 🐱 twah

4

English four

French quatre

Say It! 🐱 kat-truh

5

English five

French cinq

Say It! 🐱 sank

6

English six
French six
Say It! 🐱 seece

7

English seven
French sept
Say It! 🐱 set

8

English eight
French huit
Say It! 🐱 weet

9

English nine
French neuf
Say It! 🐱 nuhf

10

English ten
French dix
Say It! 🐱 dees

About the Translator

Golriz Golkar is a children's author, editor, and translator living in France. She loves to read books and sing songs with her young daughter who speaks both English and French.